T0157761

Undeleted

Undeleted

by
Shaheen Asbagh

authorHOUSE®

AuthorHouse™
1663 Liberty Drive
Bloomington, IN 47403
www.authorhouse.com
Phone: 1-800-839-8640

© 2012 by Shaheen Asbagh. All rights reserved.

No part of this book may be reproduced, stored in a retrieval system, or transmitted by any means without the written permission of the author.

Published by AuthorHouse   07/06/2012

ISBN: 978-1-4772-4378-7 (sc)
ISBN: 978-1-4772-4377-0 (e)

Library of Congress Control Number: 2012912270

Any people depicted in stock imagery provided by Thinkstock are models, and such images are being used for illustrative purposes only. Certain stock imagery © Thinkstock.

This book is printed on acid-free paper.

Because of the dynamic nature of the Internet, any web addresses or links contained in this book may have changed since publication and may no longer be valid. The views expressed in this work are solely those of the author and do not necessarily reflect the views of the publisher, and the publisher hereby disclaims any responsibility for them.

Dedication

To the late Ronald Graham

A Diary

And the sky brought those birds
Yet the reflection left
It's weary trace
At a natural pace
And the wings raced
The news reached home
Where nature beholds
The turbulance of a day
Where somber lies don't pay
The mother nature would say
I come to hold you
I find a way too
And soon the love will brew

A Hurdle

Hell I'll find a way
It's not over yet
I'm gonna come through
All I can say if I knew
But it's all real and new

My way is the way
And I can't give up
Now is the time
Pulse and rhythm are mine
Mom and dad are fine

One last time
Call me fresh
Front and back
One day or some day
And I will live today

OK, it's about buy or sell
Wishing well and live to tell
Through the times that last
Among the moments that we cast
If I try to tell more and bicker
The cloud in my mind'll be thicker

A Tale

The final thought
At which site
Upon what's caught
With love and might

The flame or glare
And all that light
With nothing to spare
Except a moment to fight

At the turn of age
In its middle
Upon the rage
Which became a riddle

The kings and presidents
Fell from the grey sky
And lines of residents
Of the land began to cry

Above All

A flock of birds begin to fly
And forever to color the sky
Between the rain and sand
Where lovers escape hand in hand

Free of burden
Lost in dreams
A portrait of heaven
Nature screams

Why do love and life
Only go together
Letting hearts join
In glory of it all, forever

Again

Think of me and think again
So long as my pains remain
Think of me and think again
Where my tears turn to rain
Think of me and think again
Until I use a cane
Think of me and think again
When at last I leave you in vain

An Ambition

One paves the way
Longer into a road unknown
A familiar sense of passage
A tender step into wit

Now imagine as it may
Place the picture full-blown
With those that are savage
deeming to comply and fit

More than some is many
Less is always worth a penny

An Ode

The plains and shores of the land
Colorful and pure as the clouds and sand
Pay your respect with ranks
Back your nation and fill the banks
Money she takes she would pay
For the needy, for roads to be laid

We stand apart from others
A stepping stone among gutters
Love thy land and defend it
Animosity of thy ire repented
Yet stay calm and remain in peace
And the constant wishing will seize

Bless the souls along with me
In all verses and landscapes you see
Behold, they are cheering all
Victory now is a close call
Persuade me before it's too late
With your respect for dignity and fate

Come people of this land
Sing with me hand to hand

The Anthem

The pain that brands them as
The legacy that leaves them as
The piracy that takes them as
The era that makes them as

Place or time have none
Yet human blood has some
Dignity, and pride leaves no
Intention, mercy or so

Hunger and despair rule
No fair man is a fool
It is this universe of ours
Undermined through these hours

Article

Sin is love
As men and as women
As stars and as the sky
Moon and the sun above

Tears are happiness
As peace and war
As child and mother
Blood and the printing press

Rudeness is prose
Steps from infamy
In depths of bigamy
About the petals of a rose

The history is a tale
Death is a hand
To destroy the land
A rhapsody in pale

Attracted

Essence of smell
The distance between images
That will hold us
Those that bind the self
Virtue, wisdom, and mecy

Essence of a smell
The distance between hearts
That will keep us
As one and loving
The skin, the shape, and the mercy

Battle

Platoons active in a vicious duty
Men after men, soldiers of the force
Set sail and prepare to be booting
The enemy, once she is off course

The infantry in full tilt
All forward to the road ahead
These glory seekers see filth
Where belies victory instead

The command is buried in doubt
Telling one from the other hand
In crucial condition and a draught
Condemn not your own band

The heros of war only tell
What's not deemed and won't sell
They ring the liberty bell
As blood runs heaven and hell

Bloom

The dawn's frenzy and the way of dark
Those days that we played in the park
Many times that I touched the leaves
The puzzles of humans, the rich and the thieves
In between bad and good
Those hot dishes of food
Even a pace in freedom
When I ruled my kingdom
I thought of hating you
Soon enough to make it through
I promised me a hundred
Time and time in hatred
Ever left in a pity
A scene not so pretty
I hate to do that
Like a bad callous cat
One thing I want to say
Help me if I may
The last thing I defy
Lord I hate to say good-bye!

Breeze

Breezes of the season
The rhythm of my years
A freudian play
Mind over matter
The frosty cells of doubt
Overcoming neutrons of emotion
This game . . . . a breeze
Mature as strands of hair

Prelude to a storm
As it begins to inform
And it follows the path
Like a beast doing the math
Farms and plains all the same
Houses and trailers brag
Sun and lazy porches lag
Its tornados are a claim to fame

That beast, stop it!
Taking away memories
Leaving life lifeless
Destroying every bit
When it flows as a wind
Ready now again to tend
Death toll becomes the story
While pictures vow such a glory

Death and fury over the earth
The toll from conception to birth

Burial of Ego

Would I go farther
Would I sit and cry
Panting for my breath
Should I dig harder

Beneath the elements
And the top of the sky
Would I see the years
Color those true segments

Yet I had the chance
From the first to the last
To live the future and the past
Watching the nature glance

Would I have done it over
Would I have else promised
Would I have felt otherwise
Would I yet deliver

Compass, gun, the spark of a lighter
Moments of truth, and the breath of a fighter

Cheers

A drop of courage
A show of carnage
A bite of pride
A mercy at one's stride
Note how men would pick a meal
Call for comfort and make it a deal
The hour glass would show
Those empty fists blow by blow
Those moments they survive
Those proud boasts that revive
Name your game and it's set
The wheel of fortune is a bet
Remind those cowards of the fear
True, it all goes down with a beer!

Crisis

Stray soul of a clown
Into the last episode
Unvailing the final code
Freeing a king of his crown

Paying in paper and coins
levies and taxes overdue
Struggle, compromise, and sue
Calling the brave men boys

Last act of ashes that calls
He who amassed the final hit
Repent as the lights have lit
'Tis the day your kingdom falls

Divorce

Past is the love that keeps me
Close to what future's quiet steps
Into the reality zone and pain
Foresee, and call my soul to be

Forget phrases of discretion
Where love is love and would be
Only if I had wings and wished
Your discreet touch and impression

A four-letter word and a scream
Once meant my fate in colors
Those which bear times and shades
In graded zealous calls to a dream

Better or worse as a naked horse
A shield that holds me heartless
As I say how pain is never felt
And when I deny I am fully on course

Driving

Place yourself in traffic
You and them in graphic
The dividing lines of the street
Keep you aware and discreet
Look no further than ahead
All signs in view and read
Search for others front and rear
Place the car in proper gear
And the road is all clear
To everywhere far and near
Signal to the left or to the right
Don't forget to stop at the light

Eternity

To Live up the hunch that years
Would indeed bring me tears
Let my youth seep the essence
Through the threshold of my deeds
Let my heart live the presence
In an overseen span of my needs

Evening

Flash of a light bulb
On its way to life
Brings a shock to my eyes
Like the edge of a knife

My love and caring for you
My place in the middle
And spring seems to play
A tuned and familiar fiddle

Night is long yet secret
Fancies of pride and passion
The length of hours run
As long and in an ill fashion

My steps start to promote
My retinas begin to zoom
At an stage so remote
The light leaves the room

Between my room and space
I search for love by every trace

Fame

Blessed by the pie
Time for joy and rye
Let them pray to your health
Wish you good life and wealth
For the antis not yeah sayers
For the nights and prayers
Let them applause and admire
Pleasing a lost desire
Icons and idols the same
It's all about money and fame

Fancy

Passages passages
Messages Messages
Passages a' passin'
Messages a' pressin'
Take time to glance
A'havin' fun and prance
Mounted on a pony
All dreams are phoney
Calling the wild
Smell of grass so mild
Makes me jitterbug
Kiss my pony and give a hug
Color my day pink and red
Until me and my pony are fed
I whisper into an angels's ear
Bring me more love and less fear
Gonna ride to the horizon
On my pony til I a' wisen

Get Down

Tambourine and guitar
Playing a song too far
Some gathered to choose
A harmony from blues
Lyricists discovered time
Singers sang and mimed
The face of this beauty sounds
Like a pulse beating its rounds
And the drummer secludes
With the rhythm he includes
This march of strangers on the sand
As three or four make up the band

Gossip

The Odyssey by Homer
The man probably a loner
Must be he thought
Why was it we fought
A few lines of praise
That hound man in a maze
His self and that truth
Bending the strong and the brute
The Sistine hand of grace
Bends the mind face to face
A few clouds of will
Could put you in place still

Grammar

Let me be with a verb
Please my desire and pain
Love thy skin and soul
I promise not to disturb
To be is to love
To be beyond and above
That which gives a hand
A verb is all I demand
Full-bloomed flowers of spring
Heart's desire and the light of flesh
My pain is a noun that does
A subject that would sing
Of all the verbs
Those which manipulate
And as being do stipulate
The pure colors emulate
Creation of a sentence
With a thought of fantasy
Bring us motion and ego
Behind the cutain of sense
The circles of drops
Betray the source
The words, in crops
Deceive the course

Harvest

Promise of a season
And the harmony
It holds to us and them
Where the tune of a breeze
Calling the dark of the night
Joins in with all vocals
That make the last year
A time of hope
And only the song bearers
Sing the pledge of our souls
And the time begins
Toward its familiar end
And season dies in fury
Again and mercilessly
Tenderly dancing the part
As much as a beat apart
From last but first in heart
its pulse so brave and smart
Yet ever pass this age of ours
Promise your unending hours

Help Out!

Limping, talking
Limping, walking
I am blind
I know you
Turning, burning
Turning, yearning
I am poor
I feel for you
You are old
You are standing
Aging, begging
Raging, sighing
You know me
You join me
You are blind
You are poor
I am ancient
I know the streets
You are my town
I am your clown

Here

There are the trees and the wheels
We come upon the favorite scene
Alas even if it passed our patience
Sustained the aura with vengeance

The dispute among the elements of nature
Become one and seem so peaceful
Pardoning our presence and intrusion
There upon the plains of delusion

The birds of a flock crowd the area
Chirping the commoners' songs
And emotion seeks its attendance
Eyeless for justice or decadence

The cart brushes the roots
A whole nine yards to the top
And absence of language tells
Why freedom cries and love sells

Hidden Grace

I will share my story and tell
A few words, a picture of truth
I will stand in the door with
A limb, a bruise, and a broken foot
Tell the beauties how I feel now
Taking a burden, a pain, a secret
Let me begin by saying how
How a man fights and forgets
Dignity becomes his home
Truth shows him the way
His lover plays the compass
And life leaves him astray
The flame of love, the chill of betrayal
How drops of wine paint the road in all
The wind of the past breezes through
The heart and soul awaits the last call
Humid lapses of dripping tears
Fall through and paint the fears
As words give a picture of truth
While conscience appears and soothes
Say, free me one last time again
Let me lie to wine in my pain
Ivory and iron, sword and comb, hands and feet
Travelling icons of a symbolic show of times
A pitch into the dark side of a tale
A man, a woman, a bunch of words and no rhymes
The stars pass the Lucifer, a journey to end
And the pains surpass the skin like a live flame
The moon calls for peace in the hour of dawn
Twilight appears with innocence and no blame
Treasure seekers, merchants of love and demons
Counting the breaths and sweat, blood and shame
The sanctuary turns grey as the sun rises
Too, the beasts in hunger and the angels in fame
Run away from the creation and call
The name of God, the greatest of all

Hindsight

Feeling that I had a guess
But truth was more of a mess
Years had done a job
Making them total snobs
Alas the end was fair
Shaking hands in despair

Morning brought me news
Of how day starts with dews
Then it hit me so deeply
Why I could sense so neatly
The odds that a poor sod
My Facebook friend on the Ipod

In dramatic form of a trace
Searching pals face to face
Come a year or so a pair
You get old and need repair
We form this world sadly
With blessings of loving madly

Home

Two bodies apart a distance or so
The fire of the hearts bring sweat
The heat of the moment apart and only
Two souls that never knew how to go
About love and talk that relate
The beloved and beholder among others
Like children's mothers and fathers
As a fetus paints a mind forth
tells the future like a hand
Like the palm from a java brand
Talks, boasts, and things of that sort
When we are an item and a promise
To live forward without a blame
Blue sky and none but green
The roses, the bird, through the screen
We will share house
Blow our nose
Kiss good-bye
Find time
And will never lie

Horoscope

The ivory queen and the pearl hunter
The men in the tavern, the chicks in the farm
Falling angels, the jogglers, and the onlookers
While the moon lives past the midnight
Morning to begin and the circus would call
The last sound of a horn, the lion's fall

Bring Zeus, Venus, and then the labyrinth
Of jupiter as the pieces begin to recall
That last evening and the lesson to be learned
More than one guess and two or three
Touches of sabres, the jewel of the Nile
They still have doubts about them all

Call of desire, and a rush of blood
Streets are flooded with shame and mud
History appears hidden, time is in a bottle
Those few men of pride are in a brothel

Humans

Humans work for brains
And brains for bread
Fallen in a painful thread

His faith less awful
Than a beast
His hunger at least

But they yet live
His home homeless
His mess a bless

Humans, I say, a wonder
Humans, I say, a game
Humans will live
Humans' shame a fame

Iran

Of men and women who spoke the word
Of a call for freedon and integrity throughout the world
Of more than one vote and tens of millions
Of legacy and a clear history for billions
Of a promise to change in 1979
Of glory and reassurance of 2009

Mercy

Did you play it fair
Or to forget me
Could you cry and stare
Find it hard to be

My hands beg you
My heart is slow
My belly empty
My head is low

Help us be a pair
Let me live one more year

Migration

Apart from my skin
And the blood surviving it
Aside from a home
And the breath that reminds it
Along the road that I travel
And the destiny that denies me
Among many that I detest
And the places that shelter them
Aside from home and work
And the short hint of relief
Around the edges of the border
Amass the contents of a folder
Atone for the sake of race
And the time to save face

Miss your kiss

Tender haste of your lip
To care until they rip

The blood dots that break
In two or three takes

Remind me to call
If it was love I fall

With all of my feelings and
While laying on the sand

Sun made you lighter
Summer makes me a fighter

I book my flight, order carnations
I am now tired of hesitations

My Town

My town is dancing, jumping, singing
Lights glowing and the moon winking
My town playing, sharing, thinking
A game or two, the phone ringing

I see the streets are full of blossoms
Madness is now gone
It is me in the sun
And I share the fun

First the heavens and then my town
Playing hopscotch for the run
In my town a fresh brew, red cheeks
All year, twelve months, fifty-two weeks

You are in my town my friend
Red cheek, alive and well
Saluting what we cannot sell
As well as spring, ... oh well

Next Time

I come but yet unprepared
I still abhor you
I think we are one item

Time keeps us alive
Time leaves us aside
Time plays this game

Next I see you again
Next I have to escape
Next you will catch me

Our presence, me and you
Will I ever make it through
The mirror still awaits
It is me it tries to race

Nothing

I ponder upon the green grass
Until the pain comes to pass

Pain and hallucination, alas
It won't ever be the same
Craving and shame
Memories turn to mass

It was once a fantasy
Cold hands and ecstasy
The creation and the creator
My beating heart and his legacy

A wish to remember
Through seasons then december
It all comes to me
This is then the way to be

Fresh upon the grass
While nothing lasts

Nothing!

One For The Money

Money always a blame
My familiar claim of fame
It is plenty bills in many
Configurations which I haven't any
And when they all fell
'tis money ringing the bell
Good news, good news
It's time to pay dues
Money would never play
Generous guests that stay
Don't go wrong
The road is long
Between and among
Money is the song

Pale and Soft

Flawless as a feather's flight
Seems sad under the light
The morning madness that mends
Tormented troubles of touch

Love, hope, my belief
Render me a last relief

Do the deed that drums
Notes near nowhere
While awaiting wordlessly
Tormented troubles of touch

Reach me at the end
Touch me, feel me, pretend!

Rhapsody

My only wish appears
As in a fight of spears
"Real" is the last word
As the hero pulls a sword
The room begins to spin
When the victor holds a grin
Our world tells us
What's all this fuss
Perhaps the pulse is final
The motion of the spiral
Occupy the space therein
Enemy holds it within
To part with me soon
Spinning around the moon
While holding the scene
Story at its peak is serene
The cause becomes clear
It is not courage but fear
The man knows! Listen to him!
Fill the chalice to the brim
I no more know best
Though sun yet traveling west
And I feel the soft flesh
Meshed in a splendour so fresh
Where am I now
Knowing not how
Begining an end to the day
To bring a change to my way

Romance

This silence of roses goes
I love you, I love you
When heart meets heart
Of a man whom the woman knows

The color of colors is white
When innocence subsides
And then two become one
Time to love, time to hide

Words in a lie echo
When they are but one
Tell me, tell her, tell all
Why we die, why we go

The remains of a love lost
Like emotions it too will cost

Rome

Aristotle's immense reflections
Glitter in the face of man
As Plato at last offered a hand
The day dialogue ran to directions

The Caesar's logic flowing
Albeit proved null and futile
The sons of Rome in delusion
And the serpent's fire blowing

Look up! Lands generations
Debatable yet a clear wit
Rules its hands and feet as fit
Makes truth of the revelations

The shrewd lapse of reason
The sons of sun and season
Branches of olive freezing
Philo in loss and treason

Sacrifice

Galloping down this stream
Familiar but quiet this day
My romance set in the dusk
I was in a dream as they say

For a man who wants love
Sky's high and the stars above

Wonderful were the rocks
Plants green as could be
Quiet flow of rain water
Easy to dream and easy to see

Searching with heart and soul
Even the devil blamed my role

A solitaire began to tell
The story of man and beast
And lovers played a part
Motion and touch filled the feast

I came upon a hill by a tree
Prayed the God to set me free

The sound of flowing water
Brought me the bless of nature
Calmed my soul and let live
I felt the sound of future

Come my son, come my son
Hope this maze be the other's fun

Desperate and lonely I forgave
Kissed the sky with a manner
Like beasts, like the slaves
Determined to fly the lovers' banner

Those who stood the pain
Will be paid in vain

But if a man best tries
To behold the meaning of love
Opens his heart to her
And awaits the word from above

"Ponder the stream as you may
Nature's word is love they say
Those drops of tear and blood
Will be washed in a holy flood"

Siege

Legends of courage and sabre
Cut the flesh with great labor
Men of no tribe and treasure
Kill the beasty cons with pleasure
Around and around sing out the hooves
The pallid faces of horses hold no groove
'Tis forward hereon with no pain to die
The plains are open fields of fear and lies
Brother don't betray your fellow brother
We are all white or black from a mother
This siege will at last end the infamy
And the numbers are less than many
The chariots and marches of the day after
Will bring memories near and thereafter
The common man yet denies with pride
The reason that shook us still hide
And then brother fight to the end
To find the truth and the message to send
Telling all generations one by one
Only glory and peace overcome under our sun

Sobriety

The tender grass
The fragile glass
And no more dreaming
Or time to pass

I felt the green grass
Cut my finger by the glass
Like a clown daydreaming
And the day will only pass

While reflections that remain
Divide between joy and pain

Solitude

Solitude of winter reveals
As the Chill blames the fields
And all the pain it yields
How the grandfather clock steals

Moments of truth and rundown
Can't one love one and no one
With the love that stands with pride
On every corner and every town

Solace always was and is
Of softness and of all
Another merchandise of heaven
There is one that was and is

The belief among hearts
The kissing and touching of parts
We thought we could in belief
Heavens! Until you turned the last leaf

Sophomore

Partial to wisdom and human knowledge
I play chess every day and attend college
With a regiment of gusto and my dailies
I also enjoy the taste of wine and Baileys
Last minutes of my leizure high
Indeed are by far the best with rye
Every theory haunts me like a bandwagon hound
Although I only like rock-'n'-roll for sound
Don't tell me what to do, it's bullshit!
Cause I'm free and hate to push it
Now calm down I'm not that bad
Only a legit' schizo and half mad

Speed

Odyssey, as a hammer pounds
Its beats of mercy, relentless
Confesses to the pain from sounds
Where space is breathless

The legacy of image appears
In fragile rays of the sun
A sudden unholy hole nears
The final destination of its run

Splendour

The light in the dark
City is calm
Night has fallen
When day lost its spark

The pigeons yet stop to fly
Take the dark in turns
To rest and to compromise
Perhaps sun-up would be dry

The sea is so close
Lonely blocks of trees
Dog walkers in the breeze
Rain caressing a carnation or a rose

The waiting seems so long
And yellow cabs are warm
I am between lines
Under my umbrella humming a song

Stepping Stone

Around the planet of the hearts
The flowing, floating parts
A man of heart and soul
Without a plan or a goal
Stepping into the fog and light
Bringing the day mercy and flight
The beast of burden would appear
To hold him innocent and clear
Writing the pulses of the noon
Reaching the night so soon
And let wine bring close
The smell of sweat to the nose
Coloring the skin like nature
Touching the members and stature
How one knows it is fine
How one could blame the time
Body and soul in rhyme
Painting the day in mime

Suave

Cerca de la ventana
Her hair sits in waves
Unlike lovers in caves
Her heart yet in action
On his every joke or reaction

Cerca de la ventana
The pace is lost on her lips
Senses run and lust tips
Like them, like innocent
Like sun, like crescent

The Game

The numbers on the board are funny
Staying calm when everyone is running
Away from the goal post
Planning thricks that worked most
Defense brags but offense does
As the cheers become a buzz
Bless the coach and the bench
Standing on the side in a trench
Struggle has exhausted the team
Eleven men strong as a beam
Let's hustle for another try
If we make it, girls will cry
They all say we deserve the cup
This will end with us on the top

The Latest

Pieces of a message I read
That news are hot today
Innocent creatures misfed
Dead in heaven on their way

Children cry for a morsel
Mothers cried and fathers fell

Calamities became the scoops
War and mutiny in front
Many have died among the troops
Trust and peace became a stunt

Now hand me the printed word
It all will be up to the Lord

Come peace in times to come
And how long to bury our dead
Pain is yet peace to some
Where sadness and mercy wed

Do put in your silver and keep up
A new day, a new man on top

The race settles a headline
The colors adorning the day
Guns upon this land that's mine
The rite that will never pay

Some thousands are dead in war
The earth is covered with tar

Crisis and human misdeeds
We lost, we forgot, paper reads

The Lazy Cats of Istanbul

Tears of freedom touch my shoulders
While the resonance becomes bolder
Landing is perfect and the sun up
That famous coffee in the cup
Traffic jumps me off my feet
The smoke wheels to the beat
I hear prayers every night
Those we thought are a fight
Trash flies and chatter plays
She dances and her steps just may
Begin the night you say
In a lazy and ridiculous way
Alley ways awaiting
Fishermen are baiting
Those minarets are tall and beautiful
Calling on the lazy cats of Istanbul

The Offer

There within the tasty cloud
And the drops of devotion and emotion
The call seems to be so loud
Finding its way through the distortion

Poor man's struggle to being-dom
And changes without intent or deliberation
Looking back at his long lost freedom
That is lost through many a generation

Those tingles of joy and abundance
Overcame his skin in spirit one sense at a time
Wordlessly eyeing his answer in defiance
The plain old word is like a mime

To be in suffrage yet past one's span
When life brings its news all in a plan

The Track

Refreshed my fancy to choose
A few parts of sound and news
I play that tune always too soon
Craving wine and a dance on the moon
Words play my tongue when I sense
It is me who lives in the past tense
Yet I hear my song so many times
Some play it with harps, some with chimes
Note by note I reckon it ends
In romance and kisses it sends
But to end a song in many ways
Lovers wait to see what it says
Yes I know that tune
It always ends so soon

Theory

I, alone, and having yet to isolate
I dream on and aid my broken heart
I, in pain, and such rude singularity
I find it to be true and cannot relate
Singular and passive as a mass
Time and time again where as I
Have never seen the true spirit
As the seasons come to pass
For I, singular and distant
Find truth in a blessing
Where I am the sole soul
And I find my image in flames
A handshake that calls my name
In place of stones, the epitaph
Let man be man, and the beast
The bird, the fish, and rodent
Yet singularity is cast as fate
My heart will hardly ache
My hands pray upward
My aim hides as it's too late
The plain truth never, in depth, plays thee
A two note song that seranades to be
The plain picture never is enough to thee
A paint brush that trembles to be
Song and picture energize a dream
A "come true" and deeper than the sea
And the hand over the lips and eyes of thee
Yet paint and sing in a Platonic spree
It can be red, blue, or green
Song and picture still energize a dream
The heart lives a lapse through a scream
And images begin to tell in a cloudy cream

War

A play now begins to tell
When a princess fainted and fell
As the prince dismounted
The history was recounted

The writings of Camus
Taste of bread and Hummus
Sweat almost did crowd
His tasteless face so proud

Words of deceit and sin
The clash of gold and tin
All men, a full infantry
Armoured, few sabred, and sentry

Here according to scripture
Rest, comrades, was only a picture!

What's up?

I find myself in doubt
Been through this bout
Placement and then a job
Or taking dues with the mob
A few here, a few there
Guys like me are everywhere
Bucks don't add up at all
One of these days I will fall
I would join my brother's keeper
Maybe ever so deeper
There is a call that I hear
Horizon in flame and end is near
Why waste a good life with worry
Don't say I can't say I'm sorry

You

Five fingers different in shape often tell
Friend from enemy so well

When I was in pain so bad
From fear and madness
Lack of pleasure and sadness
It was you that I really had

My moments wasted in sin and tear
My day was frightful alone
Pain was here and blame was prone
Until I found you near

That evening you were real
I felt your body and skin
In search of others akin
Love would vow and deal

And I felt your fingers
As a man who lingers
To be cured once and for all
I know it was you who answered my call

Young And Old

May you bring us sound
Our lost hopes best be found
A pause for the better
In sound, soul, and to the letter
There are only one or two
For me, while the rest is for you

Adoring the silence on the moon
And this noise will die soon
Place my desire apart
Looking up and away is smart
This crowd is now blessed with joy
Rich and poor play with the same toy

A gypsy has read the palm
That our hearts would calm
To lay the road ahead
Those good wishes that spread
The notes throughout a song
telling the right from wrong

The sound echoed deep
For young and old to reap
May you bring us sound
Our lost hopes best be found